SIMON WINCHESTER

WHEN THE

EARTH SHAKES

EARTHQUAKES, VOLCANOES, AND TSUNAMIS

VIKING
Published by the Penguin Group
Penguin Group (USA) LLC
375 Hudson Street
New York, New York 10014

USA * Canada * UK * Ireland * Australia
New Zealand * India * South Africa * China

penguin.com
A Penguin Random House Company

 Smithsonian

This trademark is owned by the Smithsonian Institution and
is registered in the U.S. Patent and Trademark Office

For Smithsonian Enterprises:
Christopher Liedel, President
Carol LeBlanc, Senior Vice President, Education and Consumer Products
Brigid Ferraro, Vice President, Education and Consumer Products
Ellen Nanney, Licensing Manager
Kealy Gordon, Product Development Manager

Smithsonian Institution
National Museum of Natural History, Department of Mineral Sciences:
Dr. Benjamin Andrews, Geologist, Global Volcanism Program
Sally Kuhn Sennert, USGS/Global Volcanism Program

First published in the United States of America by Viking,
an imprint of Penguin Young Readers Group, 2015

Copyright © 2015 by Simon Winchester, Penguin Group (USA) LLC,
and Smithsonian Institution

LIBRARY OF CONGRESS CATALOGING-IN-PUBLICATION DATA IS AVAILABLE
ISBN: 978-0-670-78536-0

Manufactured in China   Designed by Jim Hoover
Set in Baskerville MT Std and Mynaruse Royale

10   9   8   7   6   5   4

FOR COCO AND LOLA.

Respect nature. Be amazed. Stay safe. © 2015, Your Grandpa.

CONTENTS

INTRODUCTION

I remember as if it was yesterday the moment that I decided to become a writer. I was curled up with a book in a tent in a remote part of western Uganda. There are stupendously high and permanently snowcapped mountains there, the Ruwenzori—the Mountains of the Moon, as they were called in ancient times—and I was employed to look for copper in the canyons that led down from their peaks. I was a geologist with a brand-new Oxford University degree from my native England. Since I was looking forward to traveling the world, this job seemed a pretty good start. So there I was in Uganda, armed with a geologist's quartet of eternal best friends: a hammer, a magnifying glass, a compass, and a bottle of acid.

Except. Yes, I loved geology. *But—* and it was a *big* but—I had long felt a burning urge to become a writer, too. Each time I climbed a mountain and gazed at the jungles below, I wanted to jot it all down and then have someone far away read about what a good time I was having.

On that fateful day in Uganda in the winter of 1966, I read a book from the local library called *Coronation Everest* by James Morris. It is about the first successful ascent of the world's highest mountain, Mount Everest in the Himalayas, by New Zealand's Sir Edmund Hillary and Nepal's Tenzing Norgay back in 1953.

The book's author was a special correspondent for the London *Times*. Though he had never climbed before, Morris managed to get himself some 25,000 feet (7,620 m) up the mountain-

Ruwenzori Mountains, Uganda.

1

Headed for the Kamchatka Peninsula in far eastern Russia, home to twenty-nine active volcanoes.

side, and was perfectly placed for the moment when Hillary and Tenzing triumphantly reached the summit. Using all kinds of secret codes and cunning wiles Morris was the first to get the news back to London, in time to be published on the morning of the coronation of England's new queen, Elizabeth II. It was a royal gift and journalistic scoop of the highest order! Reading Morris's thrilling account and recognizing that this author's work seemed to allow him

to travel the world, I decided, there and then, right in my little tent, that I wanted his job. I wanted to be him. I wanted to swap geology for journalism, and change the direction of my life in a profound way.

I wrote to Morris, asking for advice. *If you think you can write,* he replied, *then do so. It is the best job imaginable. You'll never get rich, but you'll have a whale of a time. Give up being a geologist. Come back to England, right away, and see what you can do.*

So I did as bidden. I went back to England and managed to get a reporter's job on a small-town newspaper where I found myself writing about science quite often, which seemed a good way of making use of my university education. I loved every minute of it. After two years or so on the local scene, I joined one of the big English national daily papers, *The Guardian.* And James Morris, who insisted on reading all of my early writings, proved an enthusias-

tic supporter. We became (and have remained) the best of friends, as my own career as a newspaper correspondent began slowly to take shape and then to take off.

For the next thirty years I wandered the world for *The Guardian* and other great newspapers. I was stationed in Ireland, America, Hong Kong(China), America again, India. I visited almost every country in the world. I covered wars and scandals, revolutions and assassinations. I interviewed presidents, kings, musicians, despots, geniuses, and film stars. I was put in prison for three months on spying charges in Argentina during the nasty little war over the British-claimed Falkland Islands. I learned to sail and traveled thousands of miles on small boats. I lived an unforgettable life, rootless and wandering and eternally content.

But then in 1998, I had an unexpected success with a book I wrote about the making of the famous *Oxford English Dictionary*. And soon afterward I decided, just as I had back in Africa thirty years before, that my life should take another profound change in direction.

Just in time for an eruption! Keeping an eye on the Zhupanovsky volcano.

3

I would leave the world of daily journalism and try instead to make a living from the writing of books.

Geology, so close to my heart, was one of the topics I chose, a natural choice of inspiration. I wrote a book about the great earthquake in San Francisco of 1906. I wrote another about the huge volcanic eruption of Krakatoa in 1883 (actually called Krakatau; the more commonly known name is a nineteenth-century misspelling). I wrote about the heroic Englishman William Smith, who had battled years of hardship and prejudice and poverty to create the world's first-ever geological map. I wrote about tsunamis and geological mayhem and bad weather so many times that *The New York Times* featured a tongue-in-cheek profile of me in their Sunday magazine under the headline "The Dean of Disaster."

That is essentially how I came to be asked to write this account of earthquakes, volcanoes, and tsunamis, in which I try to knit these three kinds of natural disasters together under a single heading and to ponder out loud the questions Why does the physical world go mad so often? How do we humans deal with these violent, terrifying, and awe-inspiring events that so dramatically upset our lives?

It is a fascinating subject on many levels. I hope, in turning these pages, you will soon come to agree. And writing about such matters today serves only to confirm my lasting belief that the decision I made that winter's night in my campsite in Uganda back in 1966 was entirely the right and proper one. I hope you will agree with that, as well.

Simon Winchester
New York

On location at a king penguin rookery in South Georgia, an island in the southern Atlantic Ocean.

WÉSTENDE JEWELLERS

EARTHQUAKES

"Felt That One, Sir, Did You?"

It was early evening in the Southern Hemisphere in September 2010 when I felt it strike. I was in a hotel room in Christchurch, New Zealand. I was walking across the room, when without warning the floor suddenly lurched up and then seemed to slope downward, forcing me to half run, half stumble across to the corner by the door.

All the glasses on top of the counter tumbled off with a sound like a crystal waterfall. The television slid and listed dangerously for just a second before the floor righted itself, tilted the other way, and then settled back into a comforting horizontal position.

For a moment everything was quiet—and then a wolf-howl of sirens went off outside. I opened the curtain and saw waves of dust rising in the glow of streetlamps. It was as if the earth was a rug and something had given it a good shake. I heard breaking glass, car alarms, the yapping of anxious dogs, and then silence once again. I sat on the hotel bed and dialed down to the front desk.

"Felt that one, sir, did you?" said a cheerful voice. "About a magnitude five, I'd say. Nothing to worry about. This hotel's designed for a much bigger hit than that. But wait a minute: Are you *bothered*, sir?"

No, I said, I wasn't bothered. It was just that what I had experienced was so, well, so *unexpected*.

"Your first time, is it? Well, you have to understand, that's the thing about earthquakes, sir," said the receptionist, a fellow I now remembered, a large young man, a rugby player, he had told me when I checked in. "You just never know when to expect them."

And that indeed is the thing about earthquakes. You never, ever know. The three types of catastrophes that are caused by violent movements within the earth—volcanic eruptions, tsunamis, and earthquakes—were all, until recently, especially devastating

Wreckage and rubble in Christchurch, New Zealand, after a powerful 7.0 earthquake on September 4, 2010.

Alfred Wegener on an expedition in Greenland in 1912-1913.

because they were completely unpredictable. But technology has recently come to the rescue in two of the three cases. Some volcanic eruptions can be predicted now, a little while before they happen. Tsunamis can, too, even though their ferocity can still cause terrible events like those of recent years in Japan and Southeast Asia. Satellites and buoys can help show the piling up of waters that follows an undersea earthquake, and though tsunamis travel terribly fast, the impact of some of them can now be predicted with variable degrees of accuracy. But not earthquakes. Not yet.

There is no doubt at all about just *why* earthquakes happen. Simply stated, it all originates with the hot material from inside the earth that is always moving restlessly underneath the giant solid plates that cover the surface of the earth. The plates float on the upper layers of moving material, and consequently they move about, too. As they shift, they nudge other nearby plates or slide over or under them. Because of the friction

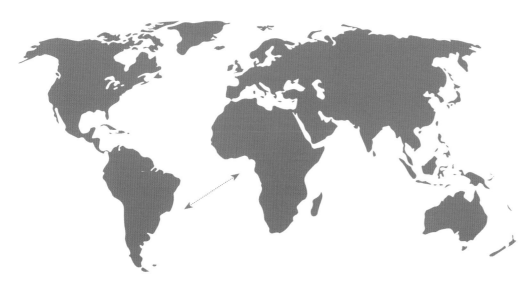

Alfred Wegener correctly noticed that the shapes of the continents fit like a jigsaw puzzle.

between two plates, great tension builds up over the years, until the tension exceeds the ability of the friction to hold the plates together, and with a terrible swift suddenness, one of the plates gives. And there is an earthquake.

The person who first started scientists thinking about the movement of Earth's plates was Alfred Wegener. Wegener was a German scientist who studied polar regions; he was one of the first people to spend an entire winter on the Greenland ice sheet—where temperatures can drop to as low as *minus 60 degrees Fahrenheit* (minus 50 degrees Celsius). Wegener also spent a lot of time looking at maps and could not help noticing, and being intrigued by, the suspiciously matching coastlines of

Africa and South America: the bulge of Brazil looked as if it just had to have fit into the space beneath what is now Nigeria. In 1912, Wegener hypothesized that these two continents, Africa and South America, must once have been connected, but at some time in the distant past had broken apart and shifted away from one another.

There were other beguiling matches that convinced him: rocks of exactly the same type had been found in Nova Scotia and across in Morocco, and in Newfoundland and across in Scotland, too. This was additional evidence, Wegener said, that these areas of land must once have been joined.

But poor Dr. Wegener was roundly denounced by the geological establish-

ment of the early twentieth century. Rocks, said his fellow scientists, were solid and eternal. Just look at the Matterhorn or Mount Everest, the geologists said. They could never move! Some called Wegener mad. He didn't get the chance to defend his theories further, because he went off to Greenland on another expedition in 1930 and died there.

But in 1965, half a century after Wegener first published his idea, a professor at the University of Toronto named J. Tuzo Wilson put together all the pieces of evidence he and thousands of other earth scientists had collected over the decades and declared that the much maligned explorer-scientist, far from being mad, had actually been entirely right: The continents *had* moved. Moreover, they were still moving!

Paleogeographers—scientists who work out what our planet's surface looked like in the past—think that three hundred or so million years ago, all the land masses on the planet were joined into one so-called supercontinent named *Pangaea* (from the Greek for *all earth*). Gradually that single mass cracked and split apart, then reformed and broke apart, again and again, before settling (albeit temporarily, for the pieces will keep on moving long after we have gone) into the oceans and continents we know today.

This ceaseless, slow movement is called *continental drift*. Continental drift has a profound effect on the earth as a whole and is the ultimate cause of many geological mysteries. Most obvi-ously, it is the reason for the look of the map of the planet, the reason that the seas and the continents were shaped the way we know them. But this eter-nal continental restlessness is also ultimately responsible for all of the earthquakes, volcanoes, and tsunamis that have for so long plagued us.

When I was at college at Oxford, I took part in one of the studies that helped prove Wegener and Wilson were right about continental drift. Six of us were dispatched on a geological expedition to East Greenland, where the rocks—

Following in Wegener's footsteps, exploring Greenland in the 1960s; I am on the far right.

mostly volcanic lavas, richly speckled with particles of iron-bearing minerals like hematite and magnetite—were known to be about 30 million years old. We trekked out on skis, hauling heavy loads of equipment on sleds we dragged behind us, and climbed up onto unmapped glaciers that probably no human had ever crossed before. Our job was to drill small samples from the mountains up on the ice cap and carefully mark an arrow on each sample showing the position of the magnetic north pole—the slowly moving point to which all magnets will swivel that marks the northern end of the earth's internal magnetic field.

When we finished our expedition and got back to England we looked at thin sections of each rock under a microscope to see which way the minute iron-laden particles inside were aligned, because since they were all tiny magnets, they would be pointing to the north pole, too—but the north pole that existed when they were laid down. What we found was that the sample particles were indeed all aligned together, as expected—*but to a point fifteen degrees east of where magnetic north is today.*

Since we knew that the pole itself barely moved—it slid around a little, and

indeed still does, but never to the degree indicated by our rock samples—there was only one conclusion to draw from what we had found: the rocks themselves, and so all of the coast of Greenland, had been shifted fifteen degrees to the west during the 30 million years since a volcano had laid the rocks down. Continents do indeed shift, and we, six college students away on a working adventure, had successfully proved it!

Alfred Wegener and I both looked at rocks for clues to how the earth works. To a trained geologist, picking up a rock or looking at a mountain cliff is like opening a history book—except that instead of reading about the history of human beings, I am looking at the history of our entire planet.

What I look at first helps me to work out how a rock might appear to have been laid down. Is the rock made up of layers, for instance, suggesting it had settled like sand from a river or the sea? Are there clues, such as new-made crystals of certain types or fragments of minerals of certain chemistries, suggesting the rock came from beneath, thrown up from the molten hot center of the earth?

The color, density, and hardness of a rock can tell a lot. Red- or white-layered rock could well be a sandstone

or a limestone, made of hardened sediments from under the sea, which is why they are known as sedimentary rocks.

Black and gray and crystalline-looking rock, on the other hand, could have erupted from deep within the earth in a molten state, only to cool and solidify later. Heavy, dense, dark rocks are often—but not always—those that come from within the earth. They are known as igneous rocks.

Some others, invariably hard and heavy complex-looking rocks, are relics of the original materials that date from the time the earth first formed, 4 billion years ago: rocks that have since been crushed and pulverized and heated and melted and remelted, the so-called metamorphic rocks.

Light, easily breakable, softer rocks may often, but not always, have formed from the sands and other rock debris swept down into the sea by rain and glaciers, or else deposited as precipitates out of the early oceans. These rocks formed much later in our planet's history—and indeed, they are all made up of worn-down bits of the old original igneous rocks.

Clues help me tell one kind of rock from another. If I can see layers in a rock, for instance, and if I know which

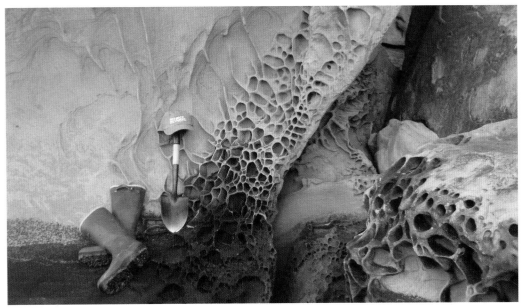

Left: Weathered limestone near Puget Sound, Washington; Right: Fossil fish and leaf, western Wyoming .

surface is the top, then it is probably safe to say that the layers on the bottom are older than the layers on the top. It makes sense. It is like making a sandwich: the piece of bread at the bottom is the first you set down, then come the layers of lettuce and ham and cheese, and then another layer on top, which is the newest. Rocks formed from the settling down of sands and debris in the sea follow the same order.

Another clue that hints at whether a rock is sedimentary is the presence of fossils, remains of once-living animals or plant life. Geologists use evidence of fossils as one way of telling how old a rock is. They know when in the millions of years Earth has existed each kind of

animal and plant lived. So if a rock is embedded with a plant fossil from 1.2 million years ago, that fossil helps scientists date the rock as having been laid down at around that time.

Where there are no fossils, no layers, and the rock is made up of an accumulation of recognizable crystals, then it is more likely to be an igneous rock. To figure out the details of an igneous rock is more difficult—though to me, much more satisfying and interesting, because I am finding out about the history of the whole earth, and not just the things that lived on it. To uncover the composition of the rock is important: I use a magnifying glass to determine what minerals it is made of. I know what they

look like, but you can easily use a rock guidebook to look up specific material, such as shiny mica or iron oxide or the kind of crystals that make up granite. When someone comes up to me with a piece of igneous rock and says, "What is it?" I take great pains to examine the rock. When I am able to say, without a doubt, that it is this or that, and is made of this and that, and then perhaps, by using specialized instruments, to measure the rock's chemistry to help show how old it is—to me, that is a moment of greatest pleasure. It is detective work of the highest order—not uncovering the commission of a crime, but the mechanics of creation.

Strata, or layers of sandstone, limestone, and shale, are part of this formation near Beulah, Wyoming.

The famous Smithsonian Institution Building ("The Castle") is made of red sandstone from Maryland.

The theory that J. Tuzo Wilson put forward in 1965, supporting Wegener's basic idea, is called *plate tectonics*. (*Tectonics* is from the Greek word for *building* or *construction*.) This theory has been confirmed by the scientific community—a confirmation to which our little expedition's geological findings contributed—and is now fully accepted by everyone. We now know there are immense tectonic plates underlying all of the continents and oceans—fifteen truly gigantic plates and about fifty smaller ones. These plates are always moving, slowly and steadily being pushed and pulled around by the hot, molten, ever-swirling rock that lies beneath them. As this endless dance shifts the plates, so it also moves the continents and the oceans that are incorporated onto the plates. And as these recognizable, named entities move—as North Africa moves northward, as the Atlantic widens, as western California slides towards the Arctic, all due to the plates moving below—so the geography of the world moves, too, always changing, never staying the same.

Specific parts of the world are particularly vulnerable to the forces of continental drift. New Zealand, where I watched the TV tilt in that Christchurch hotel room, is one of them.

The country is made up of two islands, North and South. Though there is some overlapping, the North Island sits mostly on top of the Indo-Australian tectonic plate, while the South Island is mostly on the Pacific Plate. Where the two plates join and rub shoulders with each other, or, in places, move up and down against each other, are the stunningly beautiful ranges of the Southern Alps, mountains all made by tectonic processes and delighting the tourists who flock to the South Island.

But mountains are only the half of it. Over millions of years, this slow colliding of the Pacific and the Indo-Australian Plates has produced not only immense and ever-growing mountain ranges but an endless pounding of very violent earthquakes. The lovely, flower-filled, old-fashioned South Island city of Christchurch, a more-British-than-Britain center of fine old public buildings and gracious homes, was still recovering from the quake I experienced in 2010 when it suffered a massive and much more deadly repeat six months later. That earthquake, one of New Zealand's worst, killed 185 people, and much of the center of what had been a beautiful city was destroyed. A cathedral that I had walked around just weeks before was damaged beyond repair.

The New Zealand earthquake was just one among thousands of such events where sudden tectonic plate movements killed people. In October 2005 some 73,000 people were killed by an earthquake in Pakistani-controlled Kashmir; in Sichuan Province, China, in May 2008, more than 70,000 people died; in April 2010 an earthquake in China's Qinghai province killed more than 2,000.

In all of these cases, the earth-shaking was part of the kind of plate movement that, as a by-product, creates chains of mountain. The great range of the Himalayas, with the famous Mount Everest, crosses Pakistan, China, Nepal, India, and Bhutan. Its peaks all gain about a quarter of an inch (about 6 mm) in height each time the pushing-together of the tectonic plates causes an earthquake down in the valleys below.

In the United States, the Rocky Mountains were pushed up from the earth's crust between 80 and 55 million years ago. The Rockies, and indeed virtually the entire continent of North America, sit on one tectonic plate, called the North American Plate. Far to the west of the Rockies lies the portion of the plate boundary that was responsible for America's

Earthquake damage in China's Sichuan Province, 2008.

most devastating earthquake, which destroyed the city of San Francisco early in the morning of April 18, 1906. That plate boundary is marked by an almost straight line 700 miles (1,100 km) long known as the San Andreas Fault, which runs from Mendocino in Northern California to Escondido near the Mexican border. When you fly over this area, you can see the long track of the fault, an unexpected straight-edge interruption in the otherwise random patterns of the landscape. All along the San Andreas Fault, the North American Plate stays more or less still, and the Pacific Plate grinds against it as it moves northward.

how the earth moves

Tectonic plates are immensely heavy rafts of rock of various sizes and densities that underpin the earth's oceans and continents. Fifteen gigantic plates and fifty or so smaller ones are the crucial building blocks that make up the surface of our planet.

The sixty-five-odd tectonic plates are not attached to each other. They can move. And move they do when hot rock upwelling from the center of the earth makes it to the mantle, that part of the planet that forms the underside of the plates. The soft, hot, malleable rock, called *magma*, rises and falls like the oatmeal in a pot on a stovetop, swirling upward when it is hot and gushing back down as it cools. This endless movement within the earth's mantle causes the plates floating above it to move, too, carried along this way and that, like boats caught on an unpredictable tide.

The earth's tectonic plates move incredibly slowly over millions of years. But they are so heavy—trillions upon trillions of tons (the planet as a whole weighs in at some 6,000,000,000,000,000,000,000 *tons*)—that when they hit each other or even just jostle against one another, they do immense damage to each other, as well as to the planet's surface above them. What happens on the surface of the earth depends on what kinds of plates hit and how they collide.

There are four basic kinds of interaction between tectonic plates; each has a different effect on the earth's surface above them.

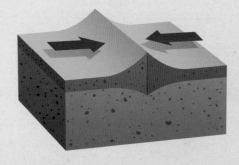

1. When two plates of similar density hit each other head-on they create gigantic piles of smashed-up rock that rise up above the surface of the plates themselves and create mountains. The Himalayan mountain chain—home to Mount Everest, the world's tallest peak—was created in just this way, when the Asian and Indo-Australian Plates collided head-on.

2. When two plates of different densities collide, then the denser plate dives under the less dense plate. This causes three things to happen. First, the rock diving deep into the mantle partially melts, because the mantle is extremely hot. Second, the violence of the colliding of the two plates causes cracks and weak spots to form in the crust above. And third, the newly molten magma down below searches out these newly made weak spots and gushes up and outward into the atmosphere. When the magma reaches the air, cools, and starts to solidify as lava, then a volcano is formed. This whole process—the diving, the melting, the crack-forming—is known as *subduction*; it is one of the basic processes in the formation of the world's volcanoes.

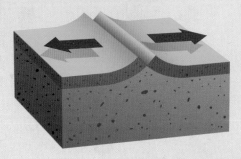

3. Tectonic plates can also pull apart from each other. When this happens, an area of weakness develops in the crust. The mantle beneath this weakness bends upward to fill in the gap, like caulk between bathroom tiles, and the melting that follows causes magma to form and ooze upward and outward. If the weakness forms under the sea, as is often the case, the magma ooze makes for small and not-very-violent (though often spectacular, with billows of smoke, steam, and ash) submarine eruptions. And from the eruptions volcanic islands form, usually several of them in a row. Such newcomers have popped up from time to time in the modern era, as a mesmerized humankind watches: a scattering have formed recently off Iceland (including the famous island of Surtsey, now half a century old, covered with vegetation, and fully a permanent part of the world's geography); some in the South Pacific (where one in Tonga was briefly named Lomu, after a popular local rugby player); others in the Indian Ocean.

4. Sometimes a plate hits another plate just slightly, like sideswiping a car. This is called a strike-slip collision. The 1906 San Francisco earthquake was caused by this kind of plate interaction. In a strike-slip collision, the two sides can be stuck fast, sometimes for many decades. Pressure builds all the time, though. Eventually the plates shift suddenly, causing a quake, long expected, but never accurately predicted.

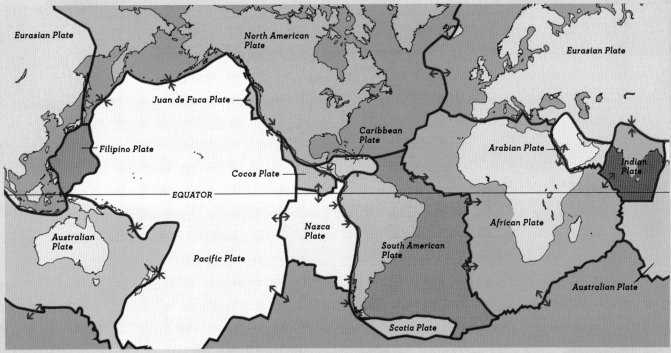

Earth's major tectonic plates.

On that spring morning in 1906, a violent shaking that lasted forty seconds knocked down buildings from one end of San Francisco to the other; fires then broke out that proved impossible to extinguish. Eighty percent of this important, vibrant city was destroyed: more than three thousand people died; three-quarters of the survivors were left homeless; the insurance costs were in the billions of dollars.

The Great San Francisco Earthquake and Fire remains perhaps the most iconic natural disaster in American history. Today, although most of the San Francisco Bay area gleams with new buildings, there are plenty of reminders of former earthquakes, if one looks closely. Most notable is a picket fence in the countryside near Point Reyes, about 20 miles (32 km) north of the city. At the point where the fence crosses the San Andreas Fault it is suddenly torn apart, with a sideways displacement of the fence posts of about *18 feet* (5.5 m). This means that at the moment of the 1906 earthquake the earth itself suddenly shifted by some 6 yards (5.5 m). That may not seem much out in the countryside where just the fence broke, but in a city crisscrossed with streets and buildings and power

People on a hillside watch San Francisco go up in flames after the quake in 1906.

The 1906 San Francisco earthquake left whole city blocks in shambles and some buildings just standing skeletons.

lines and gas mains and water pipes, a 6-yard shift can and did cause utter devastation.

San Francisco has experienced thousands of earthquakes since, most too small to feel. Though seismometers are the only devices able to detect them, and seismographs, with their pens and steadily unrolling paper drums, the only devices able to record them, a very few of the temblors are big enough to cause noticeable changes or damage. A 1989 autumn quake, though modest by historic standards, killed sixty-three people in the Oakland area and ripped a hole in the Bay Bridge, the essential route from the peninsula of San Francisco to the rest of California. A car plunged through the rift in the bridge into the water hundreds of feet below, killing the driver. Afterward, it was widely accepted that the bridge would not survive a bigger quake and that a replacement had to be constructed. Today, rising close beside the old Bay Bridge is an immense new state-of-the-art suspension bridge. It is said to be, if not wholly earthquake-proof, at least built to survive the kind of shake that all geologists are certain will one day hit the Bay area.

Will one day hit. But which day?

That's the problem. Earthquakes, whether in the United States, New Zealand, Japan, Sumatra, Chile, or China, are just not predictable.

Years of the most intense geological study have shown *where* earthquakes are likely to occur. But what people really want to know is *when*. They want to be told, accurately and dispassionately: *Will there be an earthquake tomorrow, or next week?* People want a seismic forecast that is just as reliable as a weather forecast. We have become accustomed to being advised on such matters as Do I need to take an umbrella? What coat do I wear? Will I need the air-conditioning?

An aerial view of the San Andreas Fault in the Carrizo Plain, an area about 100 miles (161 km) northwest of Los Angeles, California. If you count its curves, the fault is about 800 miles (1,300 km) long.

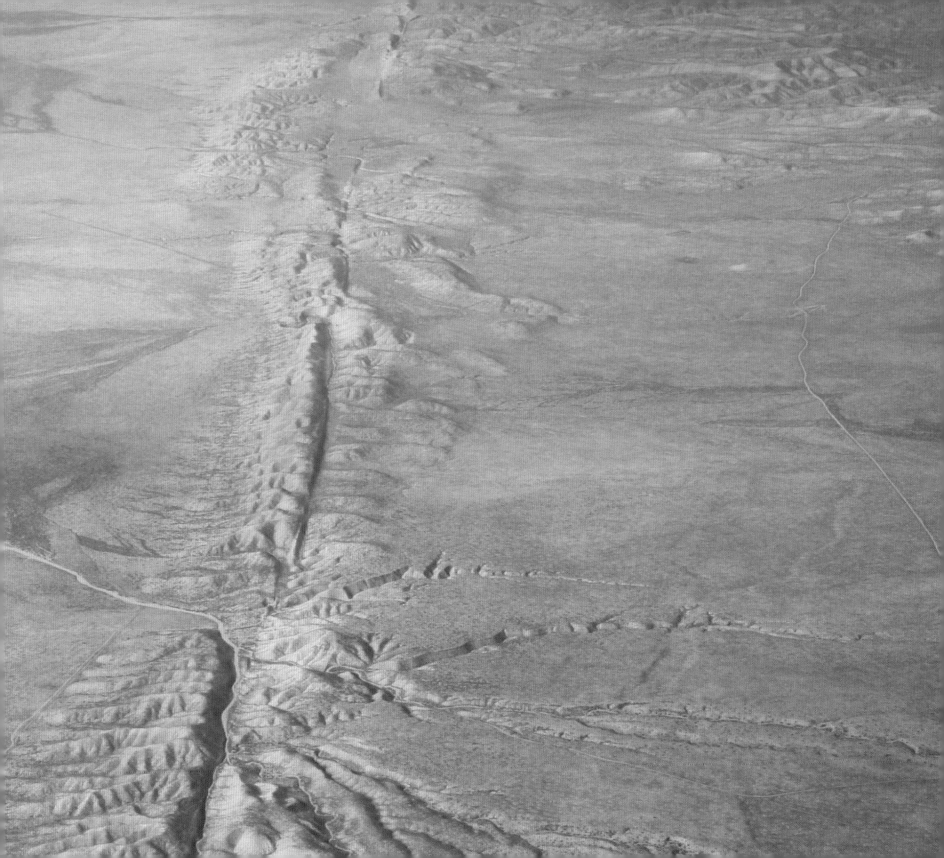

Now, in shake-prone areas of the world like California, people want to have the same kind of advice about earthquakes. Is it safe to go out tomorrow? If there is a temblor, how big will it be? Will it break the china in the kitchen? Will the freeway bridge hold during rush hour? Will any buildings come down?

So far, despite all the knowledge, all the technology, no one can give such answers. But professionals are trying!

An immense amount of scientific research is devoted to earthquake studies. Much of the work is being carried out in a tiny California village called Parkfield, more or less halfway between San Francisco and Los Angeles. Parkfield lies directly on top of a section of the San Andreas Fault that happens to be moving slowly all the time, and geologists want to know why this might be, and what causes it to move.

They have drilled a hole directly into the fault, using an oil company's rented drilling rig. They have peppered the surrounding hills with sensors and lasers that show how the hills on either side of the fault are sliding past one another, if only a tiny bit, every single day. These sensors are hooked up to observers all over the world. When I was in Parkfield, I spoke by phone with a group of geologists in Israel who were

Parkfield, California: A laser bounces off distant reflectors to measure movement in the San Andreas Fault.

measuring the shifting of the California hills. They, like scientists all over the world, are gripped by the mysteries of the earth's behavior and want to understand what is happening deep down below, and why and when sudden seismic movements occur as they do.

Outwardly there is little to be said in favor of earthquakes. They are terrible, unexpected, devastating, frightening convulsions in the ordinary order of the world. Once felt, an earthquake is

never forgotten. And yet, in part simply because they are so unexpected, earthquakes do have a way of bringing out the best in people, especially in helping to bring a shattered community together. Video footage taken moments after the February 2011 Christchurch quake, for example, shows instant gatherings of people—young, old, men, women, all strangers to one another—working together to free people trapped in their cars, under buildings, or by broken beams and chunks of masonry. It is as though people forget that they could be in danger and come together to help their community. It is a phenomenon always seen after earthquakes, and it is a heartwarming part of what is otherwise a grim and tragic experience.

Earthquakes are spectacular, awe-inspiring phenomena that are an inevitable part of the planet's behavior. They are also the events that result in the creation of some of the world's most spectacular scenery. Every time you see a beautiful range of mountains, remember what giant, violent, dangerous forces created those mountains in the first place. They were made by immense planetary forces. And forces that, so far, cannot be predicted. That is why, just as it did for me in that hotel room in New Zealand, even the smallest earthquake comes as a shock, and a reminder of the awesome and pitiless power of nature.

Sometimes that power is invisible, as when nature strikes unseen from below, with plate-shifting earthquakes. But then again, sometimes that power is all too visible, coming from high above, when great cone-shaped mountains suddenly erupt in spectacular ways.

Volcanoes.

measuring earthquakes:
THE RICHTER SCALE

There are about 500,000 detectable earthquakes on Earth each year. Only about 100,000 of them can be felt.

In order to describe and compare earthquakes, scientists use a variety of scales to measure the size and potential hazard of an earth-shaking event. One scale, invented in 1934 by a scientist from Ohio named Charles Richter, has become world famous. You hear of a quake "measuring 4.9 on the Richter scale," and you know it is fairly small, but "a 9.4 on the Richter scale" is devastatingly big. The scale below is an approximation of a Richter scale, which suggests the risk posed by earthquakes of various intensities.

	#	
	10	Extraordinary
Chile, 1960: 9.5 Alaska, 1964 : 9.2	9	Outstanding
Sichuan Province, China, 2008: 8 and 7.9	8	Far-reaching
San Francisco, California, 1906: between 7.7 and 7.9	7	High
Qinghai Province, China, 2010: 6.9 Christchurch, New Zealand, 2011: 6.3	6	Noteworthy
	5	Intermediate
	4	Moderate
	3	Minor
	2	Low
	1	Insignificant

VOLCANOES

I Bade Him Farewell

The clear, crisp final Sunday in September 2014 presented a perfect opportunity for hikers on Japan's second-largest volcano, Mount Ontake, to experience the magnificence of the fall foliage. All had believed the mountain, like nearby Mount Fuji, was dormant. But without warning Ontake suddenly exploded, and stunning images of the eruption taken by terrified climbers—more than fifty of whom died, engulfed in glowing ash clouds—went viral, speeding around the globe, reminding an awestruck world of just how magnificent and lethal truly great volcanoes can be.

In the world of great volcanoes, the name Krakatoa is legendary. The word has passed into the general language: it signifies something terrific and terrible, all-powerful, awesome, and dangerous. It is in fact the name for the greatest, wildest, loudest, and most lethal volcano to have erupted in modern recorded human history.

Krakatoa was a pyramid-shaped stratovolcano, one of the big bad boys of the volcanological world. It killed forty thousand people. The immense explosion on the morning of August 27, 1883, by which this volcano finally utterly destroyed itself, could be heard 3,000 miles (5,000 km) away. Its effects were felt and later seen by billions of people around the world.

Krakatoa, or Krakatau as it is locally known (the more widely used spelling comes from a London newspaper misprint), was originally a small island in the Sunda Strait, the busy shipping lane that separates the much larger main islands of Java and Sumatra. Today all these islands are part of Indonesia, now the most populous Islamic country on Earth; back in 1883 the islands were known as the Dutch East Indies and were run as a colony from Amsterdam, 6,000 miles (almost

September 27, 2014: Volcanic ash spews from Japan's Mount Ontake.

10,000 km) away in the Netherlands. Dutchmen administered a grand total of some thirty-seven thousand East Indian islands, of which Sumatra and Java are by far the largest.

The tiny island lying between them in the Sunda Strait began erupting in May 1883. A lighthouse keeper a few miles to the island's south saw fire and flame and smoke billowing from the summit. He used flags to signal a routine warning to passing ships, but felt no need to issue a more urgent alert, since the island was now uninhabited (it had once had a prison on it), and was only occasionally visited by Sumatrans looking for firewood. In any case, the keeper thought, this small eruption and the minor earthquakes associated with it didn't suggest the likelihood of anything worse.

But throughout the following days, matters on the tiny island did get worse . . . and then suddenly *very much* worse. Columns of smokelike ash began to rise 4 miles (6.5 km) into the air, and detonations from eruptions were soon loud enough to be heard 100 miles (160 km) away in the colonial capital, Batavia (today the giant city of Jakarta, capital of Indonesia).

Batavia in the nineteenth century

THE ISLAND AND VOLCANO OF KRAKATOA, STRAIT OF SUNDA, SUBMERGED DURING THE LATE ERUPTION.—[SEE PAGE 614.]

The caption of the September 29, 1883, edition of Harper's Weekly reports the news—and misspells the name—of the Krakatau/Krakatoa eruption.

prided itself on being a fashionable city, filled with elite Europeans eager to show themselves off as the aristocrats of the East. Their first reaction to the sputtering from the tiny island that summer was to complain about the clouds of choking dust, and that their clothes got unusually dirty. The townsfolk also objected to the increasingly thunderous noise that was disrupting their concerts. An exceptionally strong noise smashed a glass window during a Bach cantata. People started to think something quite serious was unfolding to the west.

At this time, a circus came to town via steamship from San Francisco. For some reason the elephant keeper, a young Scotswoman, decided to allow a somewhat sensitive baby elephant under her charge to sleep in her hotel room and then left it one evening while she went out to party. Krakatoa put on a major display that night, and the volcanic roaring upset the young one-ton animal, which promptly went berserk and destroyed the room; woman and elephant were summarily dismissed from the hotel. The city was getting edgy.

Right: So did the Royal Society of Great Britain in their report, "The Eruption of Krakatoa, and Subsequent Phenomena" (1888), which included this color lithograph. The report says it is based on a photograph taken on May 27, 1883, of the early stages of the eruption.

Early in August, a Dutch military surveyor, a man of either exceptional bravery or foolhardiness, took advantage of what seemed a brief lull in the activity and landed on the island in the Sunda Strait. Traveling in a tiny boat, he first passed nervously under the sheer cliffs of the islands that surrounded Krakatoa, the remaining walls of an older and much larger volcano that had erupted here some hundreds of years before. The surveyor then made a landing on the steaming, ash-covered, and now quite treeless main island, and spent part of a day walking from one end of it to the other, a distance of about 3 miles (about 5 km). He noted the presence of two huge cones, and no fewer than twelve other smaller cones called *fumaroles*, all busily spewing clouds of steam and ash, with a few tongues of flame licking out into the hot tropical air.

The military surveyor was the last human being to set foot on Krakatoa. Sixteen days later, after another steady buildup of activity, an enormous volcanic eruption utterly annihilated the island.

The catastrophe began on Sunday August 26, when a black cloud of ash suddenly rocketed into the sky, soaring more than 10 miles (16 km) high. Ships

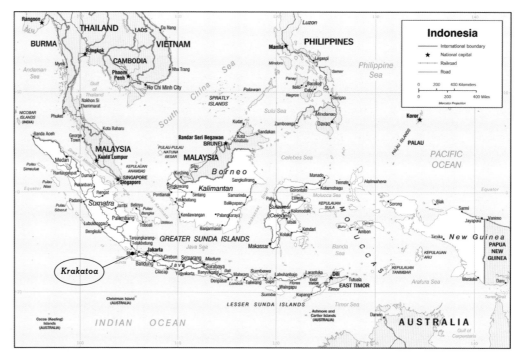

Map of Indonesia.

in the Sunda Strait reported balls of hot pumice falling from the leaden skies, a near-constant roaring, and huge waves from detonations that were being felt every ten minutes.

But there was much worse to come.

The next day, Monday August 27, shortly after five a.m., a series of four titanic explosions began, each one more violent and destructive than the last and each, according to witnesses, sounding like the end of the world. The noise was terrific, unbearable: sailors on the ships in the strait had their eardrums burst by the violence. People down in Australia, 2,000 miles (3,000 km) away, reported hearing the detonation. More incredibly, the crew on a British warship over 3,000 miles (5,000 km) away across the Indian Ocean heard the sounds and thought it was naval gunfire.

Damage was vast, unimaginable. People in the coastal villages of Java and Sumatra frantically tried to run ahead of the glowing clouds of volcanic debris; many fell and were burned to death in an instant. Chinese workers digging out a quarry 50 miles (80 km) away on Java were inundated by water—and the wall of water thrown up by the eruption was a classic example of a *tsunami*, which caused tens of thousands of deaths in the surrounding area. A patrolling Dutch warship close to the volcano was lifted up by the wave, carried miles inland, and smashed down in the jungle, with all aboard killed instantly (the rusting ruins of the ship were still visible more than a century later). Searing clouds of what was probably glowing ash and molten rock blanketed the coastlines of both Java and Sumatra, 20 miles (32 km) away, killing uncountable numbers, their bodies atomized, never to be found.

And the dust! Ash from explosions that were equivalent to two hundred million tons of TNT speared right up into the very stratosphere, as much as 30 miles (50 km) high. For a while, volcanic dust obscured the sun and helped lower the earth's average temperature by as much as 2 degrees Fahrenheit (17 degrees Celsius).

Though much of the ash and dust fell right back to earth, the smallest crystals and microscopic glassy particles from Krakatoa's self-destruction re-mained suspended in the air for months, carried along by the jet stream (the very existence of this atmospheric air current was discovered as a result). The materials in the upper sky caused weirdly lurid sunsets, which astonished the entire world. William Ascroft, a painter in London, captured the brilliant oranges and purples of the Thames-side evenings, which lasted well into the winter of 1883; the Norwegian painter Edvard Munch's famously haunting

One of hundreds of sketches of vivid post-Krakatoa sunsets by William Ascroft (1832-1914).

work *The Scream* has a swirling multi-colored background, almost certainly the Krakatoa sunsets that affected the evening skies over Oslo at the time he painted.

The impact of the August 26 and 27, 1883, eruption of Krakatoa goes well beyond the purely physical trauma of the catastrophe, horrendous though that most certainly was. One example in particular remains especially memorable.

It came as a result of the heroic efforts of a Lloyd's insurance agency's telegraph operator in Anjer on West Java who witnessed the first explosion and was able to get off a single stark sentence transmitted in Morse code to his head office in the capital city. "All gone: plenty lives lost." The line then went dead as both the operator and his telegraph office were obliterated by the blast. But the signal itself got through—and its arrival in Batavia coincided with the opening of a brand-new technology linking the Javan city to the world: the undersea telegraph cable.

Within moments the five-word message had been transmitted westward: it swept below the waves from Batavia to Singapore and then on to Penang, proceeding in seconds under the Indian Ocean to Colombo, in what

One of several versions of The Scream *painted by Edvard Munch (1863–1944).*

is now Sri Lanka; then up through the Arabia Sea to the Suez Canal and on into the Mediterranean; thence by way of the cable relay offices in Malta and Gibraltar to a telegraph station in Cornwall, Great Britain, and thence to London and to Lloyd's offices, and thanks to a special financial arrangement, to the offices of the London *Times*, then the most authoritative and powerful newspaper in the world.

The five-word message arrived at the sub-editor's hands within hours after the eruption. It was edited, arranged, confirmed, and expanded into a full news story, which ran on the main news page of *The Times*, and was read by thousands over breakfast the next day.

By contrast, news of the assassination of Abraham Lincoln on April 15, 1865, not even twenty years earlier, had taken twelve days to reach London. But now, readers in Britain, and then in America and South Africa and all over the world, were able to read news about Sumatra, Java, the Sunda Strait, and Krakatoa—all hitherto unfamiliar places—within moments. *The global village*, as it would come to be called, an entirely new concept for human society, was born—and all because of a faraway natural disaster.

After the four titanic eruptions of

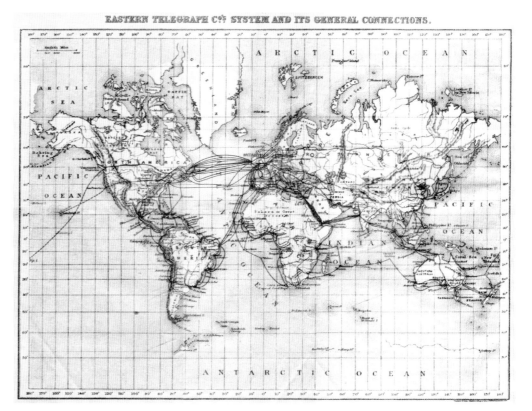

This chart of underwater telegraph cable routes shows the global reach of telecommunications at the beginning of the twentieth century.

August 1883—which history records as just a single blast—it was realized that almost all of the island of Krakatoa had vanished into thin air, utterly obliterated by the detonations. For a long while, nothing further happened. Volcanically speaking, seismically speaking, the local scene quieted. Then a mere half century later, something quite remarkable occurred.

In 1927, a group of fishermen casting their nets near where Krakatoa had been were suddenly horrified to see torrents of steam and fire roaring, incredibly, *out of the surface of the sea itself*, right where the island used to be. Steadily a sandbank grew—swept away by the tides, returning, swept away again—and then took hold. More small eruptions took place, and foot by foot, an island rose into being: Anak Krakatau, "the child" of what today's Indonesians call Krakatau. Anak Krakatau has been growing steadily

View of a mostly underwater volcanic eruption on the island of Anak Krakatau (Child of Krakatau), Indonesia, late 1920s.

ever since, a new volcano born out of the old. At the time of this writing it is well over 1,000 feet (over 300 m) high, and covered with jungle. The first grasses had begun to sprout within days of its creation; the first creature noticed there was a spider, presumably dropped by a passing seabird. Now, life in all kinds of forms has found its way to the island, including ferns and fungi, pine trees, bugs, rats, and snakes.

People are generally advised not to land on Anak Krakatau, since it is erupting more or less continuously—and occasionally very dangerously (from time to time bus-size chunks of rock are hurled out from its crater). I landed there once while researching a book. A local fisherman agreed to take me out on his boat. Once ashore I trudged and half slipped my way up the black sand of the new mountain-

side; sand that was so hot it charred the soles of my climbing boots. The crater was filled with smoke, and occasionally, if a gust of wind blew the smoke away, I could see inside the red bulging mass that burped and sputtered. Every so often the volcano sent up a lump of rock or lava that boiled over the edge or shot up in a cloud of embers.

On my return from looking down into the boiling crater I rested for a while in the cool of a patch of jungle by the beach . . . only to be confronted by a giant swimming monitor lizard that looked for all the world like a monster dragon. I threw him my chicken sandwich; he took his eyes off me and eventually swam away.

―――――――

A map of the volcanoes in the world shows, first, that most volcanoes, like Krakatoa, are found at the intersections of large tectonic plates, and second, that the great majority lie at the edges of the Pacific Ocean, at the margins of the Pacific Plate. The black triangles that indicate volcanoes on the map below are scattered around the world but clustered close together to form a horseshoe shape from New Zealand up through Japan across the foggy bleakness of the Aleutians Islands to North America and then down the west coast to the Patagonian tip of South America. There are about 450 volcanoes in this Ring of Fire, about 75 percent of all the visible volcanoes on Earth. (It has to be remembered that volcanoes are not always aboveground. Many are part of mountain ranges on the ocean floor—and very many of these are active.)

Not all of the volcanoes on this map are active. There are three phases of volcanic activity: active, dormant, and extinct. An active volcano is erupting now or has erupted during recorded time. A dormant volcano is presently inactive but is likely to erupt again, just like Mount Ontake, which did so lethally in September 2014. The third type, extinct, is a volcano that is not likely to erupt in the foreseeable future.

Wherever volcanoes are found, their level of activity is described by a scale that measures from nonexplosive to mega-colossal. (To be clear: the scale known as the Volcanic Explosivity Index measures eruptions, not volcanoes; it tells of occurrences, not of where they occur. So one speaks of the Krakatoa *eruption* in 1883 as having a VEI of 5, not of Krakatoa itself having such a thing.)

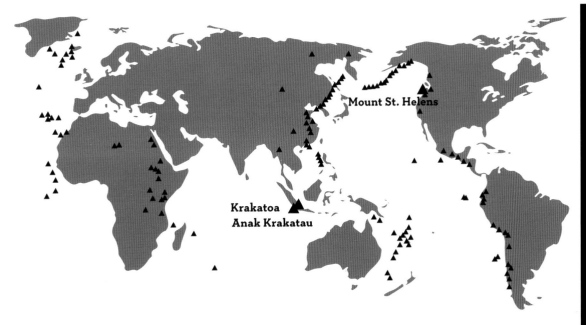

Mount St. Helens

Krakatoa
Anak Krakatau

VOLCANIC EXPLOSIVITY INDEX

0 nonexplosive
1 gentle
2 explosive
3 severe
4 cataclysmic (Mount St. Helens)
5 paroxysmal (Krakatoa)
6 colossal
7 super-colossal
8 mega-colossal

Anak Krakatau erupting during a tropical storm in July 2009.

There are many thousands of volcanoes dotted around the world, and they are generally grouped by geologists into four types.

Craters of the Moon Lava Field, Idaho.

CINDER CONES

Relatively harmless cinder cones, in which piles of lightweight air-filled and pumice-like cinders accumulate around a crater, rise in many cases no more than a few hundred feet high, and rarely cause major problems to humans or their buildings nearby. Mount Tabor in Oregon, the little-known Mount Zion in Illinois, and the volcanoes at Craters of the Moon Lava Field in Idaho are cinder cones.

Mauna Kea, Hawaii.

SHIELD VOLCANOES

The vastly larger shield volcanoes are generally also fairly low rising, but by contrast very wide spreading. They are mountains of accumulated lava that have over the years oozed and spewed their initially very liquid and then steadily solidifying magma in ways that are more spectacular than lethal. Mauna Kea in Hawaii, Eyjafjallajökull in Iceland, the Greek island of Santorini, the burping and bubbling low mountains of the Congo, the volcanoes of the Galapagos Islands, and the lower parts of Mount Erebus in Antarctica are all examples of shield volcanoes. They are beautiful

and exhibit the processes of the planet in an orderly kind of way. Providing one doesn't get too close and get burned by the lava or asphyxiated by gas, these are the safer kind of volcano, if such a thing can be said to exist.

Mount St. Helens, Washington.

LAVA DOMES

Lava domes, the third kind of volcano, are much steeper confections of lava, made of a slightly different kind of molten rock that is very viscous and thus doesn't spread so far. Lava domes tend to be quite discrete, sharp-profiled, and of all the volcano types, perhaps the least predictable. Mount Unzen in Japan, the infamously dangerous Mont Pelée in the Caribbean, and Lassen Peak in California are all examples of lava domes. And inside the crater of Mount St. Helens since its eruption in 1980, a lava dome has been growing like a monstrous carbuncle and might one day explode . . . violently.

STRATOVOLCANOES

And there are the stratovolcanoes, built of layer upon layer of old erupted lava, which display a combination of the other three types of volcano, and which are the biggest and generally most dangerous volcanoes of all. The majority of the world's most notorious volcanoes are stratovolcanoes: Fuji in Japan, Cotopaxi in Ecuador, Vesuvius and Etna in Italy, Stromboli in the Mediterranean, Mayon in the Philippines, Mount Mageik on the Alaskan Peninsula, Mounts Hood, Rainier, and St. Helens in the American northwest, and Krakatoa—or what little is left of it—in Indonesia.

Mount Mageik, Alaska.

I have climbed many volcanoes over the years: Mount Mayon in the Philippines, Vesuvius and Etna in Italy, Santorini off mainland Greece, and the infamous "gateway to hell" below ancient Hekla, in Iceland. For me the most memorable ascent was in the late spring of 1980, when I took off to see an eccentric recluse named Harry Truman, who came to his suitably dramatic end near the summit of modern America's most notorious volcano: Mount St. Helens. I was working for a British newspaper at the time: Harry Truman was famous around the world, and my editors wanted an interview.

Mount St. Helens, a 2-mile-high (3-km) peak in the southlands of Washington State, is one of a chain of great volcanoes in the Cascade Range that dominate the landscape of America's Pacific Northwest. From Lassen Peak and Mount Shasta in Northern California to Mounts Baker and Rainier up close to the Canadian border, the line of snowcapped giants stands like protective sentinels, brooding and majestic. They are the surface evidence of a 1,000-mile-long (1,600-km) subduction zone where the Pacific Plate plunges slowly beneath the North American Plate; these mountains mark the most volcanologically active part of the lower forty-eight states, as dangerous a phenomenon as it is dramatic.

And Mount St. Helens is, or least recently has been, the most dramatic of the peaks in the range. It exploded with terrific violence in 1980 and created what remains the most catastrophic example of rampant volcanism in the United States in all the country's modern history. Those of us who witnessed it, or who played some small part in the events leading up to the eruption, will never forget it. And it killed poor, defiant, legendary Harry Truman.

The first stirrings of the mountain in 1980 were noticed early on March 15 when seismographs in the local office of the United States Geological Survey (USGS) picked up abnormal signals indicating that something—probably magma—was moving, deep inside the volcano. This was most unusual: the lava dome at the mountain's 9,677-foot (2,950-m) summit had been formed fully three centuries before, and the last time Mount St. Helens had shown any activity at all was in the 1840s. Now, clearly something was happening . . . and when matters began to spiral out of control five days later, there was bewilderment and hesitancy about just what to do. Modern America had never experienced the beginnings of a devastating volcanic eruption.

Five days after the first stirrings there came a small but rather serious earthquake just to the northwest of the summit, a quake strong enough to trigger a number of avalanches in the mountain's snowfields. Seismic shocks started coming on fast and then swarming: some ten thousand small quakes were measured over a period of a month, incontrovertible signs of coming catastrophe.

Cracks began to appear in and around the summit dome, and steam started blowing out of the fractures. By late March, explosions on Mount St. Helens were occurring almost hourly, sending steam clouds—which were white-colored, and so did not have a particularly alarming look—2 miles (3 km) up into the atmosphere. But then in early April these clouds, ominously, started to blacken, and dust began to fall on towns and villages to the north and east of the volcano.

Moreover, measurements from afar showed that Mount St. Helens's shape was changing . . . *rapidly!* Up on the northeast side of the peak, a bulge developed, a huge area of rocky puffiness

The bulge on Mount St. Helens, shown right before the big eruption on May 18, 1980.

beneath which, it was assumed, a large body of molten magma was accumulating, putting an intolerable strain on the structure of the volcano. At this point the government acted.

Dixie Lee Ray, the governor of Washington who by happy chance was also a PhD-holding scientist, agreed with the USGS forecasters that it was likely the mountain was on the verge of a monumental eruption. Just like Krakatoa, Mount St. Helens is a stratovolcano, a large, pyramid-shaped accumulation of lavas from hundreds of big previous eruptions. History suggested that if it erupted again it would be a dangerous and massive event. There was, Governor Ray decided, no option but to close the mountain down.

Her decision provoked anger and howls of dismay from the hundreds of people who kept holiday homes on the mountain's cool and green lower slopes. It also prompted howls of disdain and derision from one Harry Truman. He had lived in his home beside the crystal waters of Spirit Lake since 1927, working as a caretaker for the Mount St. Helens's Lodge at Spirit Lake, a seasonal hotel north of the summit of Mount St. Helens. Truman knew and respected the mountain; all the fuss was of no consequence, he declared: Mount St.

Harry Truman—RIP—at home on Mount St. Helens.

Helens was not going to blow, and he wasn't about to be moved. It was his home; he had lived on the mountain for fifty years, and he would die on the mountain.

The old man would never know just how right he was.

The state police arrived and tried in vain to persuade Truman to leave. Then heavy wooden barriers were erected on the approach roads, and all visitors were turned away, leaving Harry alone up on the mountain. Just him and his sixteen cats.

I saw Harry Truman a few days before the eruption. I managed to get through two sets of barriers, though it was plainly dangerous to do so. When I arrived at Truman's mountaintop home, he didn't look in the least concerned. He insisted that we stand for a while at his front door, drinking in the magnificence of it all, gazing across the lake. Still, mindful of where I was, I got his story as quickly as I could. Then I bade him farewell and drove off to the supposed safety of Portland below, leaving poor Harry to his fate.

Four days later the mountain went berserk.

At 8:32 a.m. on May 18, an otherwise quiet Sunday, seismometers detected a sudden and very large earthquake. Observers trained their telescopes and saw to their horror that the quake had triggered a huge landslide on what had been the suspiciously bulging northeast side of Mount St. Helens. The shaking went on for perhaps thirty seconds, and as it continued the bulge exploded. A giant cascade of rock began moving steadily down the rock face, exposing the underlying body of half-molten magma and gas-rich, steam-rich rock that had been building up inside the volcano. It was by far the largest landslide in recorded American history—and it immediately had the most savage of consequences.

The pressure of the overlying rocks that had kept that ominous swelling in check for the previous weeks was now suddenly released. The result: an almighty explosion as millions of tons of rock and ash and molten material were hurled horizontally in an explosion a mile (1.5 km) wide, raging out of the northern side of the mountain. The blast blew out faster than the landslide itself, and so observers witnessed

An aerial view of Mount St. Helens's violent eruption.

an extraordinary sight: a gigantic land-slide of existing rock being overtaken by a carpet of newly erupted material that howled across the north side of Mount St. Helens and over the lake and forests that lay in its path.

"Vancouver! Vancouver!" cried out a voice over the radio. "This is it!" The USGS scientists in their monitoring headquarters in the town of Vancouver, just north of Portland, realized in an instant that it was their colleague, thirty-year-old David Johnston, radioing in from his observation truck 6 miles (10 km) from the volcano. These were his last words: he was overrun in sec-onds, presumably killed in an instant by the searing mass of magma and solid rock hurtling down the mountainside. The melted and mangled remains of parts of his truck were found a dozen years later. His body lies buried and unfound; his survivors can draw some comfort, perhaps, from knowing that his remains have been eternally inte-grated into the new-formed St. Helens mountainscape.

David Johnston, who is justly re-garded today as a hero by his geolo-gist colleagues, was one of fifty-seven victims of the largest volcanic explo-sion in American history. A photogra-

Charred trees and flattened timber on the mountainside.

pher, Reid Blackburn, also died, and so did Harry Truman, buried with his house and all the lakeshore properties he had looked after for so long, under hundreds of feet of ash and lava and charred trees.

The explosion itself released the energy equivalent of twenty-four mega-tons of TNT, destroying everything within an 8-mile (13-km) radius of the summit in an instant. But that wasn't the end of it; then came the rest of the eruption. Fiery avalanches of scalding dust and streams of hot mud

and melted glacier water and steam all cannonaded off the ruined peak, spreading turmoil and disaster for miles. The tumult left a 23-mile-long (37-km) swathe of destruction in which millions of trees were flattened and burned, and scores of feet of new rock were laid down in seconds.

Had the government not stepped in to close the mountain down, thousands would have died. As it was, the Mount St. Helens disaster affected millions, killed untold thousands of animals, briefly disrupted, damaged, or crippled

Yakima, Washington: 150 miles (240 km) from the blast, covered in ash from Mount St. Helens.

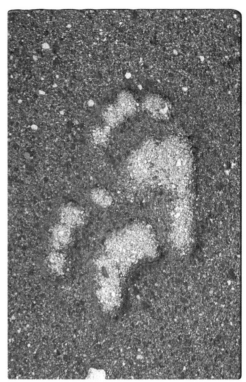

Left: Member of a USGS survey crew measuring the mudflow damage from Mount St. Helens; Right: Bear tracks in volcanic ash.

economies of towns as far away as the Dakotas and Oklahoma, and spread a dust cloud that circled the world in the following week.

Without all the warnings and precautions, the human casualty toll could have been a great deal worse. And this reflects a simple new reality: the eruption of big volcanoes like Mount St. Helens can now be forecast with some degree of accuracy *if we deploy the proper instruments.*

Volcanologists, those who study volcanoes, are essentially detectives. They investigate volcanoes to discover the history of this planet, to find out how Earth works, and to attempt to predict when one of its many volcanoes may erupt. Volcanologists collect initial information by:

● detecting and recording earthquakes, because an earthquake is an early warning signal that something energetic is happening underground. Seismometers and seismographs are the machines that measure and record movements within the earth.

● measuring even the tiniest changes in the shape of a volcano's surface, because before an eruption, a volcano may start to bulge like Mount St. Helens did. Extremely sensitive instruments called *tiltmeters* measure these changes at the surface of the earth.

● detecting, collecting, and measuring gases that are released as the result of volcanic eruptions. These gases can cause acid rain and air pollution, deplete the protective ozone layer around our planet, and contaminate soil. Since eruption plumes rise high in the air, the gases may travel far from

Mudflow carried this boulder, about 30 feet (9 m) in diameter, downstream, where it made a handy surveyor's platform.

the volcano. A small machine called COSPEC (correlation spectrometer), measures the most dangerous of the gases, sulfur dioxide.

• comparing thermal images, heat pictures, from plane and satellite flyovers. From this, scientists can tell which volcanoes are getting hotter and which lava flows are newest. The newest ones are the hottest.

• continually updating 3-D maps of areas around active volcanoes to be sure they can predict where lava might flow during an eruption. Volcanologists relate this information to national and local government agencies so they know which towns might need to be evacuated if the volcano erupts.

• and, as what is generally their first task, studying the remains of volcanic activity, the rocks and other materials that are brought to the surface, to gather clues about how a particular volcano behaved in the past. *The Present*, says the mantra which underpins all of geology, *is the key to the Past*—and for volcanologists, the flip side is true: the study of past activity may give clues to the likelihood of future eruptions.

Using the data that began to accumulate after those first stirring of seismic activity beneath Mount St. Helens in March 1980, the men and women of the USGS proved that they were able to forecast what would eventually happen; and the state and federal governments listened to what the wise ones had to say, and they acted. It was as well that they did.

But nearly one hundred years earlier in the Dutch East Indies in 1883, no such comforting forecast could be made. Krakatoa's titanically destructive end came as a terrible surprise, or more precisely, as two terrible surprises. First there was the eruption itself. And then, far worse, the event that occurred just a short while later, which killed most of the forty thousand people who died that day.

The total effect of Krakatoa was so truly tragic because the eruption spawned modern history's first recorded giant sea wave, one of the most deadly catastrophes: a vast, unstoppable rolling waterborne killer long known by its Japanese name, *tsunami*.

TSUNAMIS

Suddenly the World Went Black

It was late afternoon in Britain, cold and clear and with a low, late December sun, and I was in my car, driving back to London after spending the Christmas holiday with my parents. I turned on the five p.m. news. "Reports are coming in," said the BBC announcer in tones of unusual gravity, "of a large wave that appears to have caused major devastation in parts of Asia."

Across in Asia it was a cool clear Sunday morning, and millions of people were beginning to think about their final workweek of 2004. Thousands in the region were not working, however, but were on vacation, Europeans mainly, enjoying their Christmas holidays on the unspoiled beauty of the Indian Ocean beaches. But on that particular Sunday morning, those who were already down on the shores saw something that was at first unusual . . . and then swiftly became utterly horrifying.

On the far horizon, a line of white sea spray and surf appeared. Ordinarily such a line would vanish, but this one didn't. It kept getting bigger. And it kept on coming. Right at the thousands of people watching it from the beaches in Thailand and India and Sri Lanka and most especially in Indonesia.

All reports that December 26, 2004, morning were much the same: A distant line of white foam on the far horizon, the water on the beach inexplicably drawing back, leaving the sands dry for hundreds of yards. The distant line of foam grew nearer, steadily and silently. It grew higher. Swimmers stood up, transfixed. A few became frightened, and they and others on the beach started to walk or run inshore, glancing back at the oncoming line of white.

The line in the ocean grew still larger and more ragged; then it started to turn green, with a white line of

December 27, 2004, Phuket, Thailand: A Buddhist statue with hands folded in a traditional Thai greeting is a sentinel amid the tsunami devastation.

Above: Ao Nang, Thailand: Fleeing the deadly wave; Right: Galle, Sri Lanka: The wreckage left behind after the tsunami hit.

curling spume at its crest. It kept coming ever closer and closer, growing in size all the while. Suddenly there was a huge roaring noise, amplified by a howling windlike sound as though the ocean was pushing a gale ahead of it.

People screamed and ran as the outermost filigrees of water from the wave face began to climb the beach. Reports from holidaymakers are also all uncannily alike: A few seconds after the retreat from the sands, the great wave itself swallowed all of the beach, swept over the harbor wall, smashed down the barrier of coconut palms, spread itself thickly over hotel lawns, flooded swimming pools, roared through the hotel itself, and like a great aqueous bulldozer, pushed out onto the street beyond. The giant wall of water then raced past the tourist shops into the town, overwhelming the slums in seconds and tearing at the shanties; it inundated the neatly laid out enclaves of big houses, pushed deep into the government headquarters and the police stations, flooding the generating equipment, the schools, the radio station, and drowning everything in its path.

Everywhere almost instantly became a river of fast-flowing black seawater, going where it liked. Nothing was sacred, nothing was spared. Cars and trucks, buses and entire railway trains were carried and twisted and submerged like toys. Utility poles crashed to the ground and buildings began to topple. People holding on to one another lost their grip and watched as loved ones were torn away into the raging torrents; 130,000 people died in Sumatra, 40,000 more on nearby Indonesian islands, 35,000 in Sri Lanka, 18,000 in India, 8,200 in Thailand (holidaymakers from all over the world among them). In Thailand especially there was utter perplexity because of all the tourists. Young men and women and children on their Christmas holiday were swimming in crystal-clear waters under cool morning blue skies— then suddenly the world went black and violent. Thousands of the tourists were from Sweden; back in Stockholm it took months for any kind of understanding to sink in.

All told, 230,000 souls were lost,

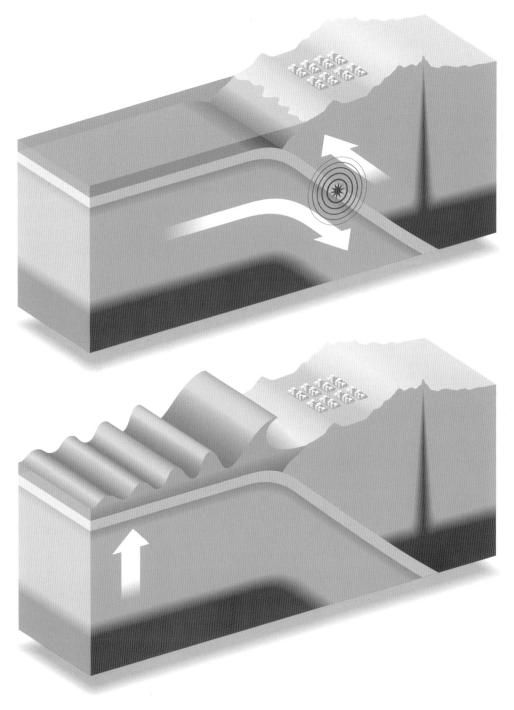

This diagram shows how a tsunami occurs if a large earthquake forces a massive slab of the ocean floor upward, which in turn pushes up the overlying water, triggering a giant wave.

most in Asia, but also on the far side of the Indian Ocean, in Kenya and Somalia and South Africa. More than a million and a half people were displaced from their homes.

The Sumatra-Andaman Tsunami, as the giant wave is now generally known, occurred on the day after Christmas, and it caught the entire planet unawares. In hundreds of places where this tsunami did so much damage and took so many lives, images of horror were caught by holidaymakers on camera and cell phone and then transmitted instantly around the world.

The ultimate event that caused the tsunami—unknown at the time, but well understood in the aftermath—was of course seismic. At about eight a.m. local time, deep beneath the sea off the north coast of the island of Sumatra, a massive rupture occurred along the subduction zone between the Indian Plate and the Burma Plate. The rupture caused a huge undersea earthquake.

It was a quake with a magnitude of 9.1—the third biggest quake ever recorded in human history. This undersea earthquake caused the whole planet to tilt on its axis. The shaking was felt as far away as Oklahoma, 10,000 miles (16,000 km) from the epicenter. And off Sumatra itself the seabed, deep underwater, shook violently for almost ten minutes. This shaking caused a huge chunk of the seabed suddenly to come detached and thrust upward; a vast, jerking movement tore out a line of undersea cliffs 800 miles (1,300 km) long, as long as the entire state of California, and forced those cliffs upward 150 feet (about 50 m), pushing the seawater above them upward and outward.

Tsunami!

About 80 percent of all tsunamis occur in the Pacific Ocean, caused by earthquakes along the Ring of Fire. Because most of the tectonic plate boundaries are under the ocean, there is a great deal of plate activity going on down on the ocean floor itself. (This "floor" is actually mountains, valleys, ridges, plains, and volcanoes. Some of the mountain peaks reach the surface. Iceland is the top of an undersea mountain, as is Hawaii.)

Weary survivors in Banda Aceh, Indonesia, walk past huge piles of debris left in the wake of the tsunami.

The study of the ocean floor is a relatively new science. It is only within the last fifty years that scientists have perfected submersibles that can reach the seabed. And that can be a long trip down! The deepest part of the ocean floor measured to date is the Marianas Trench in the South Pacific Ocean at 6.6 miles (11 km) deep, though that depth is unusual. Still, much of the ocean is about 2.5 to 3 miles (4 to 5 km) deep. The environment down there is the harshest on Earth. Darkness, cold, and the enormous pressure of the weight of water mean that the organisms that live there are unique.

The Alfred Wegener Institute (you remember Wegener from the earthquake chapter; he's the man who first expressed the idea that the continents might once have been one land mass) operates the Ocean Floor Observation System. Cameras in steel cages are lowered to a few feet above the ocean floor and towed across it capturing photographs every thirty seconds, which contribute to one massive photographic image of the still mysterious underwater world—a world that is so clearly very important for us to understand!

It is not always an undersea earthquake that causes a tsunami. The eruption of the great volcano at Krakatoa in 1883 triggered such an event, too. In this case most of the island was thrust upward by the explosion, and for a brief while its disappearance left a huge ragged hole in the ocean itself—but a hole with a white-hot core of molten magma at its bottom. Trillions of tons of seawater then cascaded into the hole. The moment that the seawater made contact with the magma, it flashed into steam in an immense secondary explosion that radiated outward into the surrounding sea, heaping the waters up and setting them spreading outward, soon to be bounced back by cliffs and other islands and fanned outward in an immense sea-green carpet of destruction to places thousands of miles around the world.

Tide gauges recorded the Krakatoa tsunami hitting Australia and the east coast of Africa; it even traveled around the bend into the Atlantic Ocean, to be felt all the way up to Morocco, Spain, and France. In southwest England the records show a tiny blip of sea-level rise, too, indicating the wave had traveled

Despite their destructive force, natural disasters were sometimes the subjects of photoprints or postcards.

The tsunami that followed the volcanic eruption of Krakatoa in 1883 washed this large block of coral up on the shore of Anyer, Indonesia.

more than 10,000 miles (16,000 km) from where it had been formed, hours before, by the eruption of a remote Indian Ocean volcano.

The highest death toll (some forty thousand people killed, most as a result of the tsunami generated by the eruption), the greatest damage, and the most colorful eyewitness accounts all occurred within about 50 miles (80 km) of Krakatoa itself. Most of the events recorded were terrible and tragic; one survivor's story, though barely credible, has become the stuff of legend. A German engineer who was managing a limestone quarry on Java 5 miles (8 km) inland, stood on top of his three-story office building, which itself stood at the top of a hill on the quarry edge. The engineer stared transfixed at the titanic explosions on the nearby island-mountain offshore when suddenly there came an explosion so vast and terrifying as to be almost beyond imagining.

And then came the wave.

The enormous wall of water steadily moved onshore. It kept on coming up the beach and over the road, ripping up cement and tearing at the iron bars of the island railroad. It still kept on, moving up across the tops of the trees, climbing and swelling until it was level with the hill on which the engineer's office had been built. The water smashed down into the quarry, instantly burying all the Chinese workers under its vast tonnage of green, and then roared on, smashing down onto the building's roof and, in an instant, plucking up the engineer and carrying him along on the surface of the wave, as if he was a surfer made of cork.

As he told his hometown German newspaper, the engineer felt curiously exhilarated by the speed at which he was carried over the jungle tops. Somewhat incredibly, he had the time and presence of mind to look to his right, where he saw all manner of broken flotsam flowing by—*including an enormous crocodile!* Fearing nothing, or maybe fearing everything, the engineer somehow scrambled onto the back of this immense reptile and, digging his thumbs into its eye sockets for stability, rode that croc like a surfboard for hundreds of yards. When the giant wave crashed and spent itself on the side of a very tall hill, he released his grip on the extremely and understandably angry animal and fled into the jungle to safety. The wave retreated, the crocodile vanished, and all that could be seen were ash clouds and steam from the distant volcano, and wreckage from the tsunami's terrible path.

The Great Wave off Kanagawa *by Hokusai.*

The Japanese gave the word *tsunami* to the world, not least because of all of us, they have had the greatest and sorriest experience of them. Although Westerners have sometimes referred to these disastrous surges of sea as *tidal waves,* they are not tidal at all. The giant waves have nothing to do with the phases of the moon and the regular up-and-down movement of the oceans.

The Japanese word *tsunami* means *harbor waves,* because they have invariably been first seen when they suddenly, unexpectedly, rushed in from the sea and completely flooded a harbor, sending all the boats, which had been thought protected, into a turmoil of raging water.

It was a Japanese painter and printmaker, Katsushika Hokusai (1760–1849), who created what's become the best known image of a tsunami, *The Great Wave off Kanagawa.* Hokusai's woodcut of a huge blue and white breaking wave bearing down on a tiny fishing boat, with the volcanic cone of Japan's sacred mountain, Mount Fuji, tiny and insignificant off in the distance, is almost as popular and well-known as the *Mona Lisa.* Hokusai created his print in the 1830s, in his old age. Although the wave pictured is often assumed to be a tsunami, it may not be, and it is unlikely that the Japanese artist ever saw one. He was probably more concerned with showing the tininess of humans under the power of the water. But Hokusai knew well how dangerous the seas were off his eternally battered island nation. Volcanoes, earthquakes, and giant waves seemed somehow to be waging an unending conspiracy of violence against Japan, more threatened and seismically affected than any other country on Earth.

A recent tsunami that devastated parts of Japan illustrates the resiliency of the Japanese people—as well as something else, something a great deal more sinister. This catastrophic event struck northeastern Japan entirely without warning in the middle of the quiet Friday afternoon of March 11, 2011. An undersea quake, magnitude 9, almost as powerful as the one that had occurred off Sumatra six years before, suddenly tore along the boundary between two shifting plates some 80 miles (130 km) off the Japanese coast. There was a huge shaking of the ground onshore—a very large earthquake certainly, but something most Japanese were grimly accustomed to. After an interval of about an hour or so, the waters that had been roiled by the quake started to arrive, in terrifying and deadly fashion, along the east coast of Japan.

The waters came quietly at first, traceries of streams that arrived almost delicately in estuaries and harbors. In footage of one small coastal town, people can be seen lingering beside a river that had unexpectedly run almost dry, CCTV images showing them walking along the promenade as they might on any cool spring day, suspecting nothing. But then the camera pans into the distance—and a line of gray *something* can be seen approaching upstream, the waters rising by a few inches and then feet, before it becomes clear that what is coming is a wave many feet high and miles long and furiously fast. Its surface is already crammed with millions of items of wreckage it has collected on its passage from the sea. And so the estuary fills, boats are torn from their mooring, huge ships are carried miles inland, entire towns are flattened, fires start, and the damage is incalculable.

Yet the Japanese people then behaved in a manner honed by centuries of exposure to such disasters. They did not complain. They did not panic. They may have witnessed immense numbers of casualties—nearly twenty

The March 11, 2011, tsunami flooded the port of Onahma in Japan's Fukushima prefecture.

*A survivor looks on at the vast destruction in Ofunato, Japan,
a few days after the tsunami hit in March 2011.*

thousand died, many more were gravely hurt—but they did not give up in the face of nature's onslaught. They did not wait for government to help. In community after wrecked community, the Japanese just went about the business of recovery, cooperating with one another, rebuilding the spirit of each town even while its very fabric was so totally ruined.

Some towns were cut off from outside help for days. When rescuers eventually reached them, they found time and again that the survivors had taken it upon themselves to do all they could. They had buried their dead, comforted their injured, and formed mini-governments to lay plans. They rationed food and medicine, found fresh water, repaired roads, cleared debris and sorted it into neat piles, reopened schools with volunteer teachers, and kept the children amused and as content as possible. The spirit of Japan in the face of a tsunami catastrophe is something that disaster planners all around the world have come to admire and hope that their own communities might use as a model.

The 2011 Japanese tsunami, known officially as the Great Tohoku Tsunami, named by the USGS for the region it hit, illustrates something else, something troubling. It shows one way in which modern seismic disasters can turn out to be much more dangerous than those occurring in earlier times, because they can damage and destroy our modern—and in this case, terribly dangerous—inventions. In Japan that March day, the invention to be so catastrophically damaged by the tsunami was a nuclear power plant.

The Fukushima Daiichi power station stood right in the path of the tsunami waves. Three of its fission reactors were running at the time of the

Above: The Japan Ground Self-Defense Force carries out work in a muddy field in Shichigahama, Japan, two weeks after the tsunami;

Right: May 26, 2012: Cleanup and inspections at the Fukushima power plant require hazmat suits and masks.

earthquake out at sea; all shut down automatically the moment sensors detected this earthquake. Enormous pumps were then immediately turned on to circulate water that would cool the reactors and keep their hundreds of tons of highly radioactive fuel stable.

But what had not been anticipated, despite a warning report issued five years before, was the inrush of tsunami water fifty minutes later—an inrushing that immediately swamped the diesel engines running the pumps. The pumps failed; the cooling water stopped circulating; the reactors began to heat up and the fuel melted; there were explosions and the release of radioactive gases. One of the world's worst-ever nuclear disasters began to unfold.

The clean up after the Fukushima accident will take many years, perhaps decades. Thousands of people have been evacuated from nearby villages while it is under way, and all because an atomic power station was built along a coastline known for its earthquakes and tsunamis, and because the station's owners played down a report suggesting that they needed to take more precautions in the event of a tsunami.

Until very recently tsunamis belonged, along with earthquakes, to the

Tsunami warnings can be broadcast from this tower on Phuket's Nai Harn Beach.

group of disasters that are not predictable. However, since the arrival of destructive tsunamis does tend to follow an observable pattern—there is a sudden seismic event, the water above the event swells up in response, and waves begin to move outward in concentric circles—it was decided, shortly after the Sumatran tragedy in 2004, to roll out a series of sophisticated warning systems.

Today, in the Indian Ocean and all other oceans, there are detection devices that will generate early warnings of possible tsunamis. Deep-ocean tsunami detection buoys, called DARTs, for Deep-ocean Assessment and Reporting of Tsunamis, record changes in the sea level in the deep ocean. Each buoy is anchored to the ocean floor. A pressure sensor on the floor measures water pressure. Readings, taken every fifteen minutes, are sent to the unit on the surface and then on via satellite to a tsunami warning center. If the sensor detects seismic movement on the ocean floor, then the machine takes readings every minute.

Tide gauges on land measure the rise and fall of the ocean level. There are thousands around the world, many that have been collecting data for many years. Information from the gauges can confirm the approach of tsunami, but the buoys provide the first information.

Tsunami warning centers on land are staffed twenty-four hours a day. They have developed efficient communication protocols for communities that may be in danger. Formulae have been written to ensure that if a pattern—an unusually sudden rise in water levels, the spreading of a wave in a certain direction, a change in pressure of the water above a sensor—is recognized, then all the islands and countries likely to be affected will be told. By radio. By cell phone. By text message. *Immediately.*

There are two existing systems in the Pacific Ocean: one based in Hawaii, another in Alaska. The Pacific Tsunami Warning Center in Hawaii did detect both the Sumatra earthquake of 2004 and the massive earthquake off Japan that struck on March 11, 2011. In this latter case they foretold the tsunami that all scientists knew would come as a result. But the warnings simply could not be issued fast enough to save Japan. Hawaii got and analyzed the signals twelve minutes after the quake. At that time, the giant rolling wave was only three minutes from the Japanese coast.

The warning system did save lives in California. The wave caused by that earthquake sped eastward across the Pacific at nearly 500 miles (800 km) per hour and took eleven hours to reach the American coast—more than enough time for the sirens to wail, for the police to issue and enforce evacua-

Left: The picture on this tsunami warning sign issues a clear message! Right: A warning center in Hawaii.

A scientist in Sri Lanka measures the height of the tsunami, using gouge marks on the tree left by debris hurdled along by the giant wave.

tion orders, for boats to be winched out of harbors, for sandbags to be put in place, for people to run uphill. Tsunamis can in theory be predicted; but if they are very big, and very close, then they will take their toll, no matter what.

Perhaps the best advice for anyone living in a tsunami-prone coastal area is simply this: Use your feet. *If you feel an earthquake through your feet, run away from the sea, and run uphill. Get to higher ground . . . now!*

Chile was hit by a giant wave in 2010, and as a consequence new construction like these elevated buildings in Concepción are being built to be tsunami-ready. The violent waters would pass underneath the building.

AFTERWORD

Earthquakes, volcanic eruptions, and tsunamis are natural disasters. And because the cost to humans can be horrifying, let us focus for a moment on the word *natural*. Each of these activities happens as a normal part of the functioning of planet Earth. Heat at the center of the planet melts rock, pressure builds, plates shift, the earth shakes, openings occur to relieve some of the pressure, magma flows across the surface of the planet, adding more rock, sometimes huge waves develop, and the sequence continues.

Scientists know more every year about where natural disasters might occur. Nothing they discover is kept a secret, so we know which areas are dangerous and when. Some people, because of economic necessity, have no choice about living in threatened areas. Those who make their living by fishing, for example, must live by the ocean. But many people choose to live in these risky areas because they can be spectacularly beautiful. Governments and businesses have hopefully learned from the Fukushima Daiichi nuclear accident not to build nuclear power plants in imperiled areas. But the temptation to do so is strong, since the plants require access to large amounts of water to cool the reactors.

All of us are conscious of the importance of protecting our planet from harm caused by humans such as pollution, climate change, overpopulation, and bioterrorism. Part of being a responsible custodian of our planetary resources must also include a respect for the way the planet itself operates. I hope that reading about my interest in and observations of what can happen when the earth shakes will increase your appreciation for the magnificent and beautiful place we call home. For its magnificence and beauty is deceptive and fragile, and over time it cannot and will not last. The impermanence will perhaps serve to remind you of what wise philosophers have been saying for many years past: *We inhabit this planet subject to geological consent—which can be withdrawn at any time, and without notice.*

At the edge of a volcanic crater on Easter Island, a remote spot in the Pacific Ocean, 1866.

RECOMMENDED READING, VIEWING, & LISTENING

BOOKS

Bourseiller, Philippe, adapted by Robert Burleigh. *Volcanoes: Journey to the Crater's Edge*. Abrams, 2003.

Furgang, Kathy. *Everything Volcanoes and Earthquakes* (National Geographic Kids). National Geographic Children's Books, 2013.

Karwoski, Gail Langer. *Tsunami: The True Story of an April Fools' Day Disaster*. Darby Creek, 2006.

Levy, Matthys, and Mario Salvadori. *Earthquakes, Volcanoes, and Tsunamis: Projects and Principles for Beginning Geologists*. Chicago Review Press, 2009.

Mallory, Kenneth. *Diving to a Deep-Sea Volcano* (Scientists in the Field). Houghton Mifflin, 2006.

Rusch, Elizabeth. *Eruption!: Volcanoes and the Science of Saving Lives* (Scientists in the Field). Houghton Mifflin, 2013.

van Rose, Susanna. *Volcanoes & Earthquakes* (DK Eyewitness Books). DK Children, 2008.

LISTENING/WATCHING

A hydrophone is a large microphone that hangs in deep water. A hydrophone 900 miles (1,500 km) away in the Aleutian Islands off Alaska recorded the earthquake that caused the Honshu tsunami in 2011. You can listen to the earthquake here: http://youtu.be/4rWDrZIucAQ

National Forest Service documentary about Mount St. Helens: http://youtu.be/3zHgwiOK3oU

National Geographic Classics: Natural Disasters DVD Collection. Washington, DC: National Geographic. 319 minutes: Contains six documentaries including earthquakes, volcanoes, and tsunamis, as well as avalanches, hurricanes, and tornadoes.

WEBSITES

Alfred Wegener Institute Gallery. A fascinating poster of images from the deep Greenland Sea: http://www.awi.de/en/research/deep
  _sea/deep_sea_ecology/time_series_studies_at_the_deep_sea_observatory_hausgarten/benthic_studies/gallery/

The Center for Disease Control and Prevention. Outline of ways to prepare for disasters: http://emergency.cdc.gov/disasters/

Pacific Disaster Center. The website of this center, which sits on the edge of the Ring of Fire, showing up-to-date maps of all natural hazards including earthquakes, volcanic activity, drought, cyclones, high surf, and flooding around the world and containing news and
  links to free disaster apps: http://www.pdc.org/

Smithsonian Institution Global Volcanism Project. A website with beautiful photographs, unrest alerts, and videos of volcanologists talk-
  ing about their work: www.volcano.si.edu

Smithsonian National Museum of Natural History, Department of Mineral Sciences. A website with all kinds of fascinating information,
  maps, news updates, and photos about geological exploration, artifacts, and exhibits: http://mineralsciences.si.edu/index.htm

U.S. Geological Survey, Earthquake Hazards Program. Earthquake photo collection: http://earthquake.usgs.gov/learn/photos.php

U.S. Geological Survey, Earthquake Hazards Program. A list of significant earthquakes around the world in the last thirty days: http://
  earthquake.usgs.gov/earthquakes/index.php

U.S. Geological Survey, Natural Hazards. An excellent overview of all natural hazards: http://www.usgs.gov/natural_hazards

ACKNOWLEDGMENTS

DESPITE THE OFTEN terrible and lethal ferocity of the earth's forces described in these pages, this book has been a joy to write and to help create. Our planet is a place of countless wonders: the drama of its making, the continuing rumbling presence below its surface, and its constant evolution inspire awe among all those who try to comprehend the geologic process. I feel sure that everyone in the team at Viking Children's Books and at the Smithsonian Institution who worked on this volume will have paused in their labors from time to time to be as amazed and inspired as I was, and as I remain. The world, and all the majesty of its making, are amply deserving of our profoundest respect.

This book was commissioned first by Don Weisberg, President of the Penguin Young Readers Group, and initially edited by Kate Waters and Catherine Frank—the latter living in New Orleans and having to shut down briefly in response to a natural disaster of a different kind, namely a hurricane called Isaac. I am most grateful to this inspiring group of three for helping to get this book off the ground.

The exciting arrangement that this book would then be published by Penguin in a partnership between Viking and the august and world-respected Smithsonian Institution, and which Viking Publisher Ken Wright announced early in 2014, brought about some changes to the editorial process, and with these changes a new editor and a much renewed energy. Sheila Keenan, with whom I then worked for the remaining months of the process, turned out to be memorable in all manner of ways: as a diligent *littérateuse*, firm in her belief that young readers deserve access to the best writing possible; as a partner with Jim Hoover, the book's incredibly skilled art director, whose choices of typeface and jacket and the internal look-and-feel of the book were invariably impeccable; as a champion of the finest illustrations, diagrams, and well-chosen pictures; and as a polite but terrier-like chivvier-in-chief, who brought me to heel and encouraged me whenever the pace slowed. She was an ever-present source of encouragement, and I was delighted to be able to work with her on a project of which, I believe, we can now all be proud. Few editors I have known in my career have ever impressed me so much, nor have been so endlessly supportive, kind, and friendly.

My wife, Setsuko, is Japanese-American. No country on earth shakes so much, nor is so tectonically affected, as the island-archipelago in the northwest Pacific that is Japan. For thousands of years the Japanese have lived with, and have patiently and stoically accommodated, the forces of nature at their most extreme and dangerous. Not for nothing is the nation's most famous symbol the great volcano of Fuji, brooding with ominous grace above Tokyo, an ever-present reminder of the primacy of the nature that created Japan in the first place.

Some of Setsuko's family live in and around Tokyo, and they and their friends both felt and suffered in some measure from the terrible earthquake and tsunami that caused such devastation in northern Japan in April 2011. Other family members live in and around the northern prefecture of Gifu, close to where a volcano, long believed dormant, erupted without warning in the fall of 2014, killing scores of innocents who were walking on its slopes to admire the seasonal colors of the leaves.

So I listen carefully and with much respect to any commentary on the geological fragility of our planet made by those of my Japanese relatives and friends whose own lives have been so endlessly affected by the earth's constant shiftings and grumblings. Setsuko-san was by my side throughout the writing of this book, offering me her constant support, knowledge, and unique insight. For this above all, I offer her my sincerest thanks and tireless devotion.

INDEX

Note: Page numbers in *italics* refer to illustrations.